Charlie

the Red-Tailed Hawk

William Grimes

ISBN 978-1-68517-634-1 (paperback)
ISBN 978-1-68517-635-8 (digital)

Christian Faith Publishing
832 Park Avenue
Meadville, PA 16335
www.christianfaithpublishing.com

Printed in the United States of America

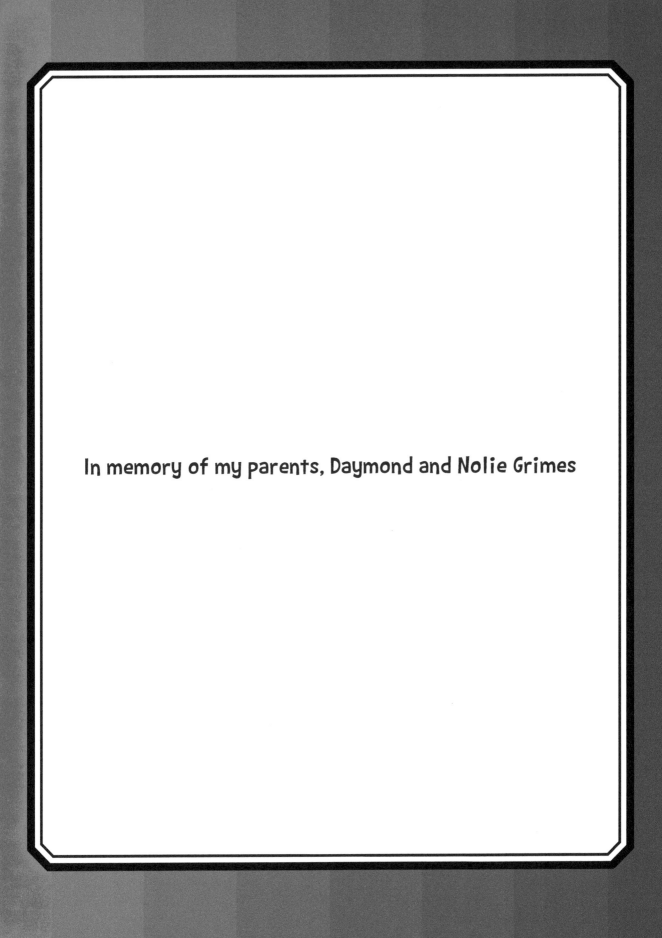

In memory of my parents, Daymond and Nolie Grimes

Acknowledgments

I want to thank Tara Tanaka, for allowing me to use her photograph of the Red Tail Hawk for the cover of my book; Heather Hill, for outstanding artwork in the design of the book cover; and Michael Hill, for answering my many questions about the Red Tail Hawks and asking Dr. Tanaka if she had a photograph of a Red Tail Hawk that could be used for the book's cover.

We lived in a little town in North Florida, thirty-five miles from the capital city of Tallahassee. The little town was called Sopchoppy. The Sopchoppy River ran next to the town, and I guess that was where it got its name.

I lived with my two brothers, one sister, and my mom and dad.

One summer morning, my dad was walking down the driveway going to get the mail. The driveway was a two-rut road, about a quarter mile in length. About halfway to the mailbox, next to a big oak tree, he saw a little bird on the ground. It looked like a hawk. At the same time he saw the hawk, he also saw a large rattlesnake moving toward the hawk. Dad knew he had to do something to save the little bird. He looked around in the ground and saw an oval-shaped rock about three inches long and weighed about two pounds. Dad grabbed the rock and threw it at the snake. The rock hit the snake on top of the head, causing the snake to turn and crawl away. Dad went over to the little bird and gently picked it up. The little hawk had broken its wing when it fell out of the oak tree. Dad carried the hatchling to the house and, using ice cream sticks and some of Mom's clothespins, made a splint for the bird's wing.

My two brothers, Earl and John, and I had been swimming in the Sopchoppy River that ran behind the house. When we ran into the house, Dad looked at us and put his finger up to his lips, a signal to be quiet. He said in a low voice, "You, boys, be real quiet and come into the dining room." We looked at each other wondering which one of us was in trouble. When we got in the dining room, we saw the little hawk with its wing in a makeshift cast. Looking at us, Dad said, "You, boys, go out to the garden and dig up a couple of earthworms. I think the little bird is hungry."

When we came back in with a couple of worms, Dad took them and put them on an ice cream stick and pushed it over to the bird's mouth. The little bird didn't eat it. Dad said, "I have an idea. I will take a stick and make it look like a bird's mouth and put the earthworm in it, and the little bird will think that it is his mother feeding him the earthworm." The idea worked and for the next month, in the afternoon, our job was to dig up earthworms for the little hawk. Dad would let us watch him feed the hawk, but we had to be quiet and stand across the room so as not to scare the bird.

My sister, Caroline, walked into the dining room one day and said we need to give the little hawk a name. Dad said, "Okay, you all get together and come up with a name."

Caroline asked, "Is it a boy or a girl?"

We looked at each other and John said, "I don't know. Why don't we pick a name that will work for either one?"

Earl said, "How about Charlie?"

Charlie was eating well (Yes, Charlie was a female. Females are about 25 percent larger than the males), and her wing was on the mend. After one month, Dad removed the ice cream sticks and clothespins from Charlie's wing. She sat on the table for about a minute, stood up, flapped her wings a couple of times, and just like that, she was gone. She flew out the window and landed on a limb in a big oak tree in the backyard and looked at six faces looking out the window at her. Over the next several years, Charlie was always somewhere close by, watching everything almost like a guardian angel.

One day, Dad was taking his daily walk out to the mailbox. As he was walking down the driveway, he noticed a large oak limb had fallen out of the tree the night before and was blocking the road. As he approached the limb, all of a sudden, Charlie came out of nowhere and flew into Dad's chest, knocking him back. Then Charlie came back around and landed in front of the log, between Dad and the log. Charlie started hopping toward Dad, flapping her wings and screeching. As Charlie was doing all this, Dad realized the problem. That same rattlesnake was behind the log, ready to strike at Dad when he grabbed the limb to pull it out of the road. Dad knew it was the same snake because it had a knot on the top of its head where he had hit it with the rock several years ago. The rattlesnake crawled off and Dad moved the limb out of the roadway, and he and Charlie walked on down to the mailbox.

As the years passed, Dad's health started failing, and Mom passed away. Dad was determined to stay at home. We all lived within a mile of his house, so we took turns checking on him. One fall afternoon, Dad and Charlie were in the garden. Dad was hoeing the weeds, and Charlie was eating earthworms. All of a sudden, Dad stood up, dropped the hoe, grabbed his chest, and fell backward, landing flat on his back. Charlie flew over to him, landing on his chest. Realizing that something was wrong, Charlie flew off. A couple of minutes later, Charlie flew through the window of Caroline's house. No small feat for a bird with a wingspan over four feet. Charlie flew through the house looking for Caroline. She found her sitting at the dining room table, reading the newspaper. Charlie landed on the table and started acting like her wing was broken. Then she would take off and fly out to the window. If Caroline wouldn't follow her, she would fly back through the window, over to the table, and pretend to have a broken wing. This time, it worked. Caroline jumped up, grabbed her cell phone, and ran out of the house and followed Charlie, all the while calling us and telling us to get to Dad's house. Then she called 911 and got the ambulance headed to Dad's house.

When Caroline and Charlie got to the garden, Dad was trying to sit up. He told Caroline that his chest felt like a mule had kicked him. The EMTs put Dad onto the gurney and loaded him in the ambulance and headed to the hospital. Caroline called Dr. Jeffers and told him that the ambulance was taking Dad to the hospital and would be waiting for him there.

Dr. Jeffers, Dad's heart doctor, was waiting when the ambulance arrived and moved Dad straight to the ICU. Dr. Jeffers put Dad in a medically induced coma so they could evaluate his condition. While the doctors and nurses were working on Dad, Charlie sat on the window ledge, looking in the window. Dr. Jeffers made a comment about the bird to one of the nurses, and she said the hawk was flying in front of the ambulance when it pulled into the parking lot, then it flew away.

We were all in the waiting room when Dr. Jeffers came in and told us that Dad was okay except for a red mark on his chest on top of his heart and that he had suffered a massive heart attack, but so far, they couldn't find anything else wrong. They were going to keep him for a couple of days and see if anything shows up. We all thanked Dr. Jeffers and headed home. The next day was Saturday, so we gathered at Dad's house to go over what had happened the last twenty-four hours. Caroline made the remark that Dad said that his chest felt like it had been kicked by a mule, so what made the red mark on his chest? While Caroline was cleaning Dad's house, John, Earl, and I walked out to the garden to look around. We walked over to where the hoe was lying, and we could still see the imprint of Dad's body where he had landed in the soft soil. Next to the hoe, lying about where Dad's heart would be, was a rock about three inches long, weighing about two pounds and in the shape of an oval. I picked it up and put it in my pocket. I asked John if he remembered Dad talking about the time he picked up a rock and threw it at the snake that was getting ready to eat Charlie.

"Do you remember where it was along the driveway?" I asked.

Earl said he remembered Dad saying that Charlie fell out of the oak tree, and there was only one oak tree along the driveway. We started walking down the driveway as Dad had done for sixty years. We stopped at the base of the oak tree and started looking around. Earl found a spot that didn't have any grass or leaves on the ground, and the ground was indented like something was missing. I reached into my pocket and pulled the rock out that had been lying by the hoe in the garden. It was a perfect match.

"Well," I said, "we know where the rock came from but how did it get to the garden?"

As we looked at the rock more closely, I noticed scratch marks on the rock.

"Do you think that Charlie realized Dad was in trouble, and before she flew over to Caroline's house, she flew over here, picked up the rock, flew to where Dad was lying, dropped the rock on his chest, and then flew to Caroline's house to get her?"

John said, "Well, if the rock matches the mark on Dad's chest, then Charlie saved Dad's life because from what Dr. Jeffers said, Dad was dead when he hit the ground and only someone who was right there could restart his heart and would be able to save him. About that time, Caroline pulled up to where we were standing and got out of her car and walked over. I said, "I think we have figured out what happened, but we need to go to the hospital. We all loaded up in Caroline's Crown Vic and headed to the hospital. On the way, I called Dr. Jeffers and asked him to meet us in Dad's room and that we would be there in twenty minutes. When we got to Dad's room, Dr. Jeffers was waiting for us. He said, "I hope this is worth getting me off the golf course."

I stood up and said, "I think we know what caused the red mark on Dad's chest."

I reached into my pocket and pulled out the rock, walked over to Dad's bed, opened his hospital gown, and placed the rock on the red mark. Perfect match.

"How did it happen?" Dr. Jeffers said. "No one was there."

I said, "Yes, there was." And I turned around and pointed to Charlie. "She was there and saw Dad fall backward, and before she flew over to Caroline's house, she flew down the driveway and picked up this rock, the very rock that Dad had used to chase the rattlesnake away when Charlie fell out of the oak tree and broke her wing. You can see the marks her talons made when she picked it up and flew back to where Dad was lying, dropped the rock on Dad's chest, and then flew over to Caroline's house. If she dropped the rock at a height of thirty feet, the rock falling would generate sixty pounds of energy or about the same amount that a fist would have, enough to restart Dad's heart. I think you doctors call that a precordial thump."

Dr. Jeffers said, "Yes, it would be possible to restart the heart if it can be done within a minute or two. That is why we use the term *witnessed arrest*. You have to be right there in order to restart it instantly."

Dr. Jeffers still could not believe it. Three days later, Dad was back home, rocking in his rocking chair with Charlie looking down at him from her tree limb. As the days passed, Charlie was getting too old to hunt for her food. Dad would buy meat and cut it into small pieces and lay them out where Charlie could find them. He would always wear rubber gloves so as not to put any human smell on the meat. Charlie was getting to the end of her life span. She was twenty years old, and Dad was eighty.

One afternoon, around dusk, Dad looked over at Charlie sitting on the table next to Dad's chair. Dad reached over and put his hand on Charlie's head and said, "Goodbye, old friend. It's been a good ride."

Dad died with his hand on Charlie's head, and Charlie never moved again. Charlie died at the same time. Charlie lead the way to heaven for Dad, and like she had always done, she was his guardian angel. We had a special casket made so that Charlie could be by Dad's side where she belonged.

The End

CPSIA information can be obtained
at www.ICGtesting.com
Printed in the USA
LVHW071611230922
729127LV00007B/156

9 781685 176341